SWEEPSTAKES SCAM
GUIDEBOOK

ROBERT ROSS

PAGE PUBLISHING, INC.
New York, NY

First originally published by Page Publishing, Inc. 2018

ISBN 978-1-64138-300-4 (Paperback)
ISBN 978-1-64138-301-1 (Digital)

Printed in the United States of America

This book will help you and save you
thousands and thousands of dollars

WHAT TO WATCH OUT
FOR THE DOS AND DON'TS
THE 1-876-000-0000
WHAT TO ASK FOR

SWEEPSTAKES
TELEMARKETERS
FALSE PAYDAY LOANS
THE LIES THEY TELL YOU

CONTENTS

ALL ABOUT SWEEPSTAKES SCAMS

Hello, my good friends, I'm here to help you out on sweepstakes scams. Have you ever sent in a sweepstakes form, fill it out from a department store, grocery store, mall, or any place that you see a display that has these form so you can fill them out and find out later that you're not getting nothing in return? And have you ever been scammed that paying out something big on a cash prize win and pay for a product and a processing fee and get nothing in return? This *Sweepstakes Scams Guide Book* will help you look out for all those scammers that tell you you're going to receive a big cash prize but pay a processing fee. I'm writing this guide book to everyone in the USA and all over the world and to protect yourself and learn what to watch out for on all the sweepstakes that's out there today. Order my guide book, and you'll be prepared on what to do and what not to do and protect yourself and your bank account and credit card numbers, etc. You'll find out once you read through my book and save your money and protect yourself so you don't have to waste your money on sweepstakes that try to say you're a winner but get nothing in return. Sweepstakes is a prize contest that you send in for and/ or a product that you purchase. They tell you you'll be a winner if you enter into a sweepstakes. Once you send in all your information like name, address, phone number, your income—and that's all it takes—they will sell your information to other companies that will take your information and start calling you and tell you, you won a cash prize under from sweepstakes. A sweepstakes is something for the scammers to make money off. You *don't* give them any important information on yourself like your bank statement, SSN, etc. Sweepstakes is an advertising or a promotion of a product by which items of value or a prize are awarded to participating consumers by chance. There is no purchase or entry fee required to win and no fees or taxes to be paid prior to receiving the prize. If any purchase or payment is required to collect winnings, then it cannot be a sweepstakes or promotion but may be a lottery. It is not possible for an event to be both a lottery and a sweepstakes. Be very careful on this. You'll find different ways to protect yourself once you read my book on sweepstakes scams.

There are other ways that they will get you involved with and talk you into a way to help you out to get your prize, like cashing checks from other people's checking account. So be careful—all their ways to do and get you in a way so your bank account goes in the negative are not true. Don't let them talk you in doing the wrong things to get your prize; they want your money and get you in a way that will get you broke. You can learn more on telemarketers, bad payday loans in my book. The best way to win is to not give them your information and your money in any kind of a way that they can get it from you and lose everything in your bank account, credit cards, personal information that can get you broke and get nothing in return, so be very careful on any of your information that's not worth it And don't let them talk you into paying their phone bill out of your pocket like a (TOP UP - PHONE CARD). You get these cards from Rite Aid, Walgreens and tell that this is to help you out to get your prize faster. Not true—it's to help them put. I want to stop them from doing this scamming to all the people who live in the world.

2

HOW THEY CALL YOU AND GET YOU EXCITED ON YOUR PRIZE WINNINGS

They call you on the phone, and they will take up your time and talk fast and get you excited on your cash winnings that they say you won. And at this point, they might tell you on how you won a big cash winnings on a sweepstakes even if you didn't apply or send in the form when receiving it in the mailbox. Once they tell you how much you won on your winning cash prize, they will avoid giving you information on their part at this time. They will tell you, "Congratulations on your winning." The more of a cash winning they're telling you, a high amount at first on your winnings, the more they want you to pay a percentage of your cash prize winnings to receive it and let you know on what you have to pay to get it. But at first, get their information like their full name, their phone number, the company name, city and state were their calling from. (THIS IS VERY IMPORTANT TO GET THIS INFORMATION FROM THEM BECAUSE IT'S NOT TRUE WHERE THEY'RE CALLING FROM, AND BE CAREFUL BECAUSE THEY'RE USING AMERICAN NAMES TO THROW YOU OFF, AND ALL OF THIS IS COMING FROM JAMAICA.) You'll learn more

in other chapters of this book. And watch out for them to keep calling you again and again—be careful. And once they have all your
information, you'll start seeing a letter on a sweepstakes that you can
alter it and pay the fee and send it in. Then after that, you have to
enter the code number on the coupon. You'll be in the big system;
they will call you over and over again and get you excited on your
winning cash prize. These people will be very pushy and will tell you
all about your winning prize that is big and it could be a first, second,
third place prize that you won. Once they call you on the phone,
they will tell you anything and lie to you on what you won. But if
you're smart enough, once they get you excited and congratulate on
your winning, they will tell you they will call you back and go to
the next step. And they will use different people to call you and to
assure you of your cash prize on your sweepstakes. They will call you
over and over again, about twenty to thirty times or more until you
answer the phone.

(DON'T FORGET THE MAIN REASON WHY THEY
KEEP CALLING YOU BACK IS ONLY FOR YOUR MONEY,
AND EVEN IF YOU DON'T BELIEVE THEM, THEY WILL
ASSURE YOU THAT YOU'RE A WINNER OF A PRIZE AND
HOW TO CLAIM IT.) They will use a different phone number to
throw you off. The phone number will also come up as a private,
withheld, unknown, restricted—and also be very careful with these
calls. They all work as a team in one big room or their own home
and a warehouse where they all work as a big team in Jamaica. Be
careful. Watch out for different phone numbers; you'll learn this in
other chapters in my book. I'm here to protect you from spending
out a lot of your money and protecting your bank account because
will they try to put it in negative amount and cause you to have your
credit cards maxed out also, and they will get you in the hole and
you'll be broke.

3

THEY TELL YOU ALL ABOUT WHAT YOU WON, HOW TO CLAIM IT

After getting you excited and congratulating you on your prize, they will tell you on the next phone call to receive your cash prize and how to claim it, what percentage to pay and to use your banking account to receive the processing fee that is the tax processing, shipping, and handling fees. If you ask a lot of questions, they will explain this amount and break it down for you and how it comes to this amount. Try not to believe this but play along like you're still excited. Later in this helpful guide. I'll explain how to get this information faxed to you as soon as possible. Tell them to get the information ready and tell them to call you back in one hour. While they're getting this information, be ready to go to the nearest office supply store or a place to receive a fax. Make sure you ask for their place of business, phone number, company name, and address. Only give them your name to receive this fax. Once you get this information, save it for your records and use it later. To claim your prize, take the amount and make it out to a name like Western Union, etc. (I'll GET TO THIS MATTER IN OTHER CHAPTERS IN THIS BOOK OF MINE.) They will provide you with a person's information. Make sure you send it to that person. Be careful were you send it to, like Jamaica and other countries as well. Once they get you on the phone, they will go over all on how much you have won. Remember, once you put your information on an entry form and your income, if you have a lug income, they will tell you your prize is big that gets to be in millions of dollars. And go over all the taxes, shipping and handling, stamp of approval, fees that you have to pay. The prize amount that they tell you about is anywhere from $2.5 million to $5.5 million, and they will tell you about two new cars you won, a new house that you won. They will also tell you on your cash prize of up to $25,000 and in between $50,000 and more than $100,000 cash that they will bring to you. And they will tell you also what you won with car insurance that is paid for you up to two years.

And they will also tell you about a credit card for one year that you can spend. Free gas card also for one year. Don't believe this because it's more money and a payment that they want to take from you. These all sound good, doesn't it? But don't believe them because your bank account will be dry all up and you'll be in debt. This is all true in my book. I've been through this and paid out a lot of money and got nothing in return but my bank account in negative, which made me broke. I paid out in between $1,000 and $5,000 that got me in debt. And I still haven't received my prize. Especially on a 1-876-000-0000 number (more in other chapters). REMEMBER, JUST BE CAREFUL ON ALL THESE. GUYS FROM JAMAICA, THEY WILL LIE TO YOU ON GETTING YOUR PRIZE TO YOU, AND ALL THEY WANT IS YOUR MONEY FROM YOU AND PUT YOU IN DEBT BECAUSE THERE IS NO PRIZE AT ALL IN THE WORLD. They will go over everything with you to claim your prize and all the other gift items you think you're getting, but you wait for them to come, but it's more lies. And once they get you to believe them about your prize and all the other gifts items, they sometime come up with an extra fee that they need for you to pay out to receive your prize, which is more money that they will try to get you to pay out, and it comes from another person who will call you and let you know it's the finale payment to claim the prize (DON'T BELIEVE THEM; IT'S ALL LIES THAT THEY TELL YOU TO PAY MORE AND DON'T PAY OUT NO MORE MONEY TO THEM).

THINGS AND PERSON TO LOOK OUT FOR

After getting the information on how much you're getting on your cash prize and the percentage needed to pay for the processing fee, different people will call you to set up the amount to get the money up on your percentage and what's next on the insurance money also for your protection. (REMEMBER IF YOU DON'T HAVE ALL THE MONEY YOU NEED TO GET YOUR PRIZE, THERE'S ANOTHER WAY TO GET MORE MONEY FROM YOU AND THAT'S WHY THEY TELL YOU ABOUT THE PAYMENT PLAN. THIS IS ALSO A RED FLAG. DON'T FALL FOR THIS AND ANYTHING THAT THEY TELL YOU TO DO.) There is another amount they want you to send to them, but this is not true at all. They say you'll get this back after you send in your processing fee to make sure you'll get the cash prize winnings. In my guidebook, I will explain how different people will contact you about the delivery of your package they say you won. They will tell you a day and time that you will receive your cash prize winnings. Be careful on this matter as more people will start calling you for additional money that they want you to pay out, each person who calls you wants a fee from you because you send it out to the first person easy and they all want some of your money like a pie. They all work together as a team and tell you who is coming to help you claim your price. For instance, they will say the police the delivery guys, the news, security guys, the prize agent, and the main guy (LIKE THE BOSS) will show up at your residence. The news people and if you like for them to show up. The scammers are con artists using the lies of a sweepstakes to convince consumers to send in money to claim a prize they supposedly won. The scammers are getting bolder, using names of the government agencies at and legitimatize phone numbers that mask where they're calling from. They're claiming to represent the "NATIONAL CONSUMER PROTECTION AGENCY" and the nonexistent NATIONAL SWEEPSTAKES BUREAU, and even the FEDERAL TRADE COMMISSION (FTC).

They say that the delivery of the sweepstakes prize is being supervised by the supposed government agency (NOT TRUE). This is scamming by convincing the consumers to wire money to a foreign country (OUT OF THE USA). They want you to send a money transfer to companies like Western Union, Money Gram, or an agent of Lloyds of London or some other well-known insurance company. The insurance money they want you to pay out for your winnings will cost you a high percentage for it to be safe so you can receive it in a safe matter and all it is for you to pay out more money to get your prize, but it's going to cost you in the thousands and thousands of dollars to get your sweepstakes prize and by then you have already paid out a lot of money, and you're not close to getting it. (IT ALL COMES DOWN TO PAY OUT MORE MONEY TO EVERYONE WHO CALLS YOU ON YOUR PRIZE.) Be careful, it's easy to believe this because that's what they like to happen to you and make you broke in your bank account and credit cards. (DON'T LET THIS HAPPEN TO YOU. I'M HERE TO SAVE YOU FROM ALL OF THIS, AND YOU'RE NOT GOING TO GET ANY SWEEPSTAKES AT ALL.) Because you'll do anything to get it, and it sounds good what they're saying to you so you can waste your money and give it to them (DON'T DO IT) and spend your money to them. I've been doing this research for seven years and have been through it all. I lost thousands and thousands of dollars over the years and got nothing of my sweepstakes. They all work as a team in a big room or a warehouse and some work in their home. They live in Jamaica.

HOW MUCH YOU HAVE TO PAY OUT, BUT FIRST IT'S A LITTLE AMOUNT AT FIRST AND WORK OUT A PAYMENT PLAN

When they tell you your prize amount is over a few millions of dollars that you won and a new house, cash money, gas card, free insurance, two new cars—that is a crazy amount each time they call you each day. The fee can be over $2,000 to $5,000, and if your prize is more the fee, it can be over $10,000 to $50,000 and up to $100,000 and after you spend out from a small fee to a large fee at a time. At first, you'll tell them you don't have that kind of money at this time. (BE CAREFUL, THEY DON'T WANT TO LOSE YOU THAT'S WHY THEY WILL WORK OUT A PAYMENT PLAN WITH YOU SO THEY CAN GET YOUR MONEY FROM YOU AND MAKE IT SOUND SO TRUE.). So they will let you know that they can work out a payment plan for you. Once you do this payment plan, like sending to a Western Union, Money Gram, and get a Green Dot MoneyPak card from Walmart, they will tell you can even do a Green Dot card. Hawaii gets more into these cards and Western Union, Money Gram I will discuss in other chapters. Now, they will tell you about your checking account and how to give them numbers off your account, but don't do this. Or a manager credit card that you have and they can use the numbers off it and get more money from you without you knowing it. So the best way to play is not to enter into a sweepstakes and you can save thousands and thousands of dollars. These are different ways they want you to send them the processing fees and amount.

6

THEY TELL YOU SOME ADDITIONAL COST LIKE TAXES, STAMPS OF APPROVAL, SHIPPING AND HANDLING, AND OTHER FEES

They will tell you all about additional cost, taxes, stamps of approval, and the shipping and handling. Be very careful with the additional cost that you have to pay out; it's extra taxes on your prize, different stamps of approval that they come up with and will tell you to pay out more from state to state when they come to deliver your prize. The shipping and handling fees that they want you to pay for and also storage fees, express fees, and a rush fees so you can get your prize sooner—don't believe these. It's just more money that they want from you so you can pay out more money to them and have your bank account broke and you still won't get your prize. (REMEMBER THESE, GUYS ARE IN JAMAICA AND JUST WANT MORE MONEY FROM YOU, AND EACH GUY WILL CALL YOU, AND YOU GET TO PAY DIFFERENT GUYS EACH TIME WHO PLAYS THEIR PART IN YOUR SWEEPSTAKES THAT YOU'RE NOT GETTING ANYWAY AT ALL.) And watch out for different guys who call you also that they are the delivery guys. They want you to pay more money. Don't believe them; it's all lies. They come up with these different things to pay out each step of the way, and they want you to believe them for everything that they tell you to pay out and to claim your prize.

7

WHAT THEY WANT YOU TO DO TO RECEIVE YOUR CASH PRIZE

The sweepstakes scam requires you to pay to receive the prize you won. The legitimate sweepstakes will never ask you to pay fees to participate or to receive a prize. You should never have to pay a handling charge, service fees, or any other kind of charges upfront to receive your sweepstakes earnings and those are sure a signs of a sweepstakes scams. Sweepstakes taxes are paid directly to the IRS along with regular tax return, except for rare occasions such as paying for port fees or hotel taxes. Sweepstakes scams and criminals instruct you to wire money using these service like Western Union, Money Gram, and also ask you to buy a Green Dot MoneyPak card because it is nearly impossible to trace who received the money. Western Union and Money Gram transfer are handled like cash, and it is nearly impossible to get back any money that you send to con artists in this way. They pressure you to act in a hurry, and they have a good reason for wanting you to act quickly to send in a payment before someone to change your mine. They want to ensure that they receive their money before their check bounces or you read an article like this one and make a decision before you have the time to ensure that the win is true and legitimate—you should be very suspicious. You'll become broke and they want you to receive it they will talk you into it even if you don't have any money to use to pay for your processing fees. (THEY WILL ASK YOU TO BORROW FROM A FAMILY MEMBER OR A FRIEND.) They will ask you that there is a way to help yourself to receive your prize they will have checks coming to your house so you can put it in the bank and send them the money back to them and cause your bank account to go negative, and also they would want you to pay on their phone and get a card from the drug store to add minutes to their phone. Be careful: don't play their game. Other examples are in my book.

8

THEY TELL YOU TO GO OUT AND GET A GREEN DOT MONEYPAK CARD

When they tell you how much money to put on a Green Dot MoneyPak card and to send it to them, they will tell you to put it on a Green Dot MoneyPak Card (GREEN CARD FROM WALMART.) The cost is $4.95 fee plus the money to put on once you do this. They will call you back and after you purchase this card, you search it off and give them the number on the back. Then they will tell you it will be processed for your prize, and then your prize will be relieved. The place where to get the Green Dot cards is at Walmart, Walgreen, Kmart, Rite-Aid, CVS just to name a few places. I'm here to help you; don't do this. Once you pay out on this card, you will lose your money and won't be able to pay it back or get anything in return. These cards, they tell you to put money on—it's easy for them to have you put it on the card and give them the PIN on the back of and take your money, and it can't be traced back; it's easy for them because they live in Jamaica.

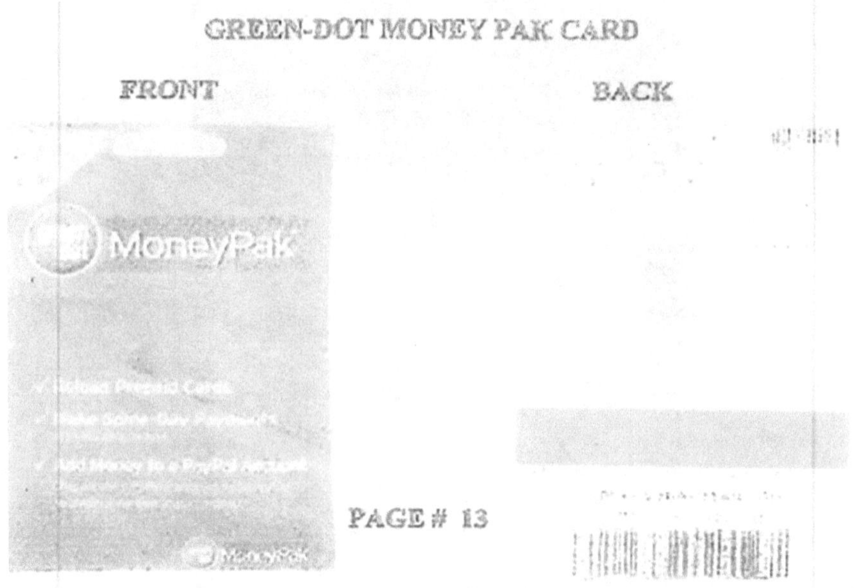
GREEN-DOT MONEY PAK CARD
FRONT
BACK
MoneyPak
PAGE # 13

Walgreens
$21.99
ezetop
No Value Until Activated At Register
Recharge cell phones
of family back home
Recargue el teléfono móvil
de su familia en su país
telcel
Digicel
top up
movistar
LIME
Claro
SMART
airtel
RELIANCE
Mobile
JAZZ
Globe
MEGAFON
MTN
For more information, see www.

ALL ABOUT WESTERN UNION AND MONEY GRAM AND A TOP-UP CARD

They ask you to send money to Western Union or Money Gram. When they tell you the amount you have to pay with all the payments you made, they will tell you where to go, to a store like Walmart, Kmart, or any kind of a store to wire payment,, and they will give you all the information to send the money to. They will lie to you about all of this because the name they give you is either an accountant or a merchant banker, and watch out for these names and people. The real bad place to send it is Jamaica. Be careful of this place—there'll be more on this in the coming chapters. These other cards such as a top-up card is used to add minutes to their phone that they ask you to get for them the reason for this is so you can get your prize quicker, but it's a lie to you and use you again to get more money from you.

You'll be broke after doing different things that they want you to do for them.

Examples

Digicel

LIES FROM DIFFERENT PEOPLE TO SEND THE MONEY

They will tell you lies from different people to send the money like an accountant, and they use their own people like family members—brother, cousin, friends and different workers that they tell you about. These family members will also claim to be accountants'. (THEY WILL CON YOU AND YOU WILL GET NOTHING.) Now partners are just the same, but they change names on each category or situation when you send money like I said before about Western Union and Money Gram. And the biggest thing is a Merchant Banker and how they say is the person who does all the main account and control all the money in the account. Once you send in all money payment, it goes to Jamaica. (BE CAREFUL ON SENDING MONEY TO THIS COUNTRY.) Some of the payment goes to USA. But this is about 10 percent because of sending money to these places. They have a call center with all agents that they call themselves. I'll get more on this situation later.

11

WHO TO SEND THE MONEY TO

They use different people for you to send the money to and you can get your prize a lot quicker like they say you're getting, but more lies. They use a middle person in the USA. And so you think that the company is there in the USA, but it's not—it all comes down to Jamaica. The middle person lives in the USA. They give some of your money to that person as a fee, and they send back the rest of it to Jamaica. They make more of about four times to about six times or more. Of the things that they say and do to get your prize and who to send the fees to. Be careful not to do any of this because you are not getting any prize money back as your winnings. (NOT AT ALL.)

ADDITIONAL WINNINGS, LIKE CARS, FREE GAS, CASH MONEY

They will tell you about additional winnings, like cars, free gas, for a year on a gas card, vacations, new home, and cash money that ranges from $50,000 to $100,000 to even a higher amount and $150,000—this is not true. The cars that they say you won is just a new car that they come up with. They will tell you, like I said earlier, to pay a bigger fee in order to get a luxury car. They even double it to get a double fee, so watch out for this. (THAT'S TWO CARS.) It'll be more money from you to give them. The free gas that they say you won is put on a gas card, and yes, there is a fee on this as well. With all these additional prizes that they say you won, it all comes up to nothing. All you'll do is pay out additional fees between all the cash prize, fees, additional prize, and get nothing in return. Don't pay out anything to them and the best way to win on a sweepstakes and don't enter one and don't pay out anything knowing that don't matter what they say to do. Keep your money and don't fill out any entry form that you see in any store.

13

TELLS YOU WHO'S COMING TO GIVE YOU YOUR PRIZE

They will tell you all about different people who're coming to bring your prize like your agent from the beginning and two security people from the company, and they say (BUT DON'T BELIEVE THEM) the UPS service or any other service that they say is coming. They will tell you that they're coming in on a private jet from your airport. They will make it sound so good for you. Be careful; it's not true. And what they bring to you as all of your prizes—your cash money, more prizes, cars that the tow driver is bringing, documents on your new home that you won. These different guys that tell you all lies because they all work together to scam you out of your money and to make you broke so don't believe them at all.

NAMES AND PHONE NUMBERS OF SCAMMERS

(1)   PAUL ANDERSON   1-876-433-5780
(2)   COOPER   1-876-366-8153
(3)   JAMES COOPER   1-876-287-8425
(4)   JAMES TAYLOR   1-876-765-5027
(5)   JOHN LEE   1-876-899-8902 /
                             1-876-506-2204
(6)   JOHN LEE #2   1-876-404-5210 /
                             1-876-445-7685
(7)   JOHN HOLLOWAY   1-876-283-1790
(8)   MARYESBELLE   1-876-256-8884
(9)   MIKE WASHINGTON   1-876-466-6164/
                             1-876-284-8804
(10) MR BELL   1-876-370-2952/
                             1-876-367-1746
(11) MR YOUNG   1-876-280-4236
(12) MRSREED   1-876-355-3479
(13) PETER MOORS   1-876-419-1712

(14) PETERSON — 1-876-473-2770

(15) ROBERT JACKSON — 1-876-583-6575

(16) RONALD CAMPBELL — 1-876-290-9143

(17) TONY WASHINGTON — 1-876-280-7239

(18) VICTORY — 1-876-562-8565

(19) WASHINGTON (CODE #1984) — 1-876-582-6327

(20) WASHINGTON — 1-876-582-6327 /1-876-490-3955

(21) WILLIAMS — 1-876-414-7218

(22) GEORGE LOPEZ — 775-410-1206

(23) JOHNATHAN — 914-298-8815

(24) JACK JOHNSON — 646-201-5306

(25) JOHN SID WELL — 214-989-6578/ 786-220-3054

(26) MICHEAL PETERSON — 518-2580-2012/ 1-876-446-6164

(27) LOPEZ — 323-786-8043

(28) PAUL CURRY — 518-795-6889

(29) CAMPBELL — 1-876-406-3544

(30) TONY EDWARD — 345-939-2940

(31) MR PETERSON — 513-286-8740

(32) PETER JOHNSON — 407-304-0669

(33) LINDA JACKSON — 702-609-9283

(34) LINDAWALLACHE — 1-876-306-8004

(35) DAVID SIMMONS — 954-284-5518

(36) JOHN HATCHER — 702-997-2379

(37) DAMON JAMES — 775-410-1929

(38) MICHEAL SMITH — 760-298-6568

(39) GEORGE McNEIL — 1-876-581-7419 / 775-410-1206

(40)	KIMBERLY FRANCIS	702-609-7061
(41)	ANDRE CROSS	1-876-450-0185/ 209-233-6738
(42)	MIKE ANDERSON	1-876-840-9958
(43)	MRS WILLIAMS	1-876-776-5027
(44)	DAVID	786-220-3197
(45)	ANDREW SAT	718-576-1989
(46)	HERMANN SALVED	440-721-1384
(47)	JOHN	786-220-3054
(48)	MARK HASTING	214-884-6097
(49)	PAUL	518-795-6889
(50)	PEDRO	919-441-5074
(51)	WAYNE CARTER	848-207-5904
(52)	MR CROSS	360-567-6680 / 718-342-2690
(53)	MR WINTER	1-876-370-2952
(54)	MICHEAL WASHINGTON	1-876-454-4874
(55)	MRMcFARLANE	415-234-9628/ 1-876-438-4268
(56)	PETER WOODS	1-876-367-1746
(57)	GEORGE McNEIL	760-992-5366
(58)	ANTONIO	786-374-2983 / 1-876-258-9820
(59)	ANTONIO#2	1-876-899-3593
(60)	DAVE WASHINGTON	1-876-440-7767
(61)	TAYLOR	1-876-340-1014
(62)	JOHN BEN	1-876-254-3569
(63)	OMAR	760-666-5600
(64)	DAVE BROWN	1-876-844-7800
(65)	WALKER	1-876-570-7368

(66) DAVE CODE NAME   1-876-798-0549
      JESUS CHRIST

HARRIS	1-876-825-9780
VIRGINA BLACK	757-509-5229 / 505-807-4006
JOHN TAYLOR	305-357-0810
JOHN BEN	1-876-505-7554
ROY RUFF	1-876-386-3513 / 1-876-442-7361
TAYLOR	214-838-9951
PETERSON	1-876-390-9907
TAYLOR COUSIN	1-876-809-5999 / 1-876-536-9543
WILLIAM LEE	1-876-386-3513
JACK	1-876-575-7718
MARK JONES / JOHN BEN	1-876-487-6772

THESE GUYS CHANGE THEIR NAMES AND NUMBER ALL
THE TIME TO THROW YOU OFF

CHAPTER # 14
(1) WINNER'S INTERNATIONAL
(2) AMERICA CASH REWARD
(3) COLOMBIA CLEARING HOUSE
(4) COLUMBIA PUBLISHER REWARD
(5) GOLDEN NUGGET RUSH REWARD
(6) MEGA MILLION GIVE AWAY
(7) INTERNATIONAL LOTTERY SWEEPSTAKES CO
(8) GLOBAL GOLD RUSH
(9) GLOBAL INTERNATIONAL REWARD
(10) WINNER PRIZE INTERNATIONAL CASH REWARD
(11) INTERNATIONAL CASH REWARD CO
(12) AMERICA LOTTERY SWEEPSTAKES
(13) GOLD WORLD CASINO
(14) GLOBAL INTERNATIONAL LOTTERY CO
(15) AMERICA CHOICE REWARD
(16) WESTERN CREDIT REWARD
(17) PEOPLE WINNERS INTERNATIONAL CO

THESE ARE ALL PHONY SWEEPSTAKES COMPANIES
THAT SAY YOU WON A CASH PRIZE AND
GIFT ITEMS

Some of these companies tell you they all come from some were in USA—not true. Not one company is true or in business. They all come from Jamaica. Be careful; it's all about lies.

15

LETTERS THEY SEND YOU

Dear Mr. Robert Ross,

I am pleased to inform you that your cheque of __________________ is now released by the ____________. This letter serves as a legal notice to you;_______________ that this is being held by the (___) under the ___________ of the betting, gaming and lottery's act. Please note that the money that you have acquired is 85% tax-free under the _____. The option is available where you either choose to receive a certified cashier's cheque or the funds wired directly to the bank via (TT) wire. For security reasons, you are advised to keep the following information confidential until you have cleared this process and your money has been transferred to "your" account.

However, the documents pertaining to the clearance of your awarded payout valued at ______ will be processed and approved by our hoard of directors along with the Attorney General and legal representatives in a meeting scheduled for ___________. To confirm and complete tin's process as representatives will instruct you on the process to receive your awarded funds. As you were told on the phone you are required to pay the customs and insurance charges amounting to (USD$895.00) before, so that we can expedite the funds promptly in your possession. This is payable through the western union or to the specified broker within the accounting department; ________________.

Thank You.
Yours truly,

Vice President

THE FEDERAL RESERVE BOARD.

NOT TRUE LETTER ABOUT SWEEPSTAKES

Dear Mr. Robert Ross,

I am pleased to inform you that your cheque of _______________________ is now released by the _____________________. This letter serves as a legal notice to you; _________________ that this is being held by the (___) under the________ of the betting, gaming and lottery's act. Please note that the money that you have acquired is 85% tax-free under the ______. The option is available where you either choose to receive a certified cashier's cheque or the funds wired directly to the bank via (TT) wire. For security reasons, you are advised to keep the following information confidential until you have cleared this process and your money has been transferred to "your" account.

However the documents pertaining to the clearance of your awarded payout valued at _____ will be processed and approved by our board of directors along with the Attorney General and legal representatives in a meeting scheduled for __________. To confirm and complete this process as representatives will instruct you on the process to receive your awarded funds. As you were fold on the phone you are required to pay the customs and insurance charges amounting to (USDS895.00) before, so that we can expedite the funds promptly in your possession. This is payable through the western union or to the specified broker within the accounting department; __________.

Thank You.
Yours truly,

Vice President

THE FEDERAL RESERVE BOARD

NOT TRUE LETTER ABOUT SWEEPSTAKES

16

PHONY CHECKS

AMERICAN CASH AWARDS 094

JANAURY 28, 2012

Pay to the Order of JOHN SIMPSON $ US 2,500,000.00

TWO MILLION FIVE HOUNDRED THOUSAND Dollars

WACHOVIA

COMPUTER BALLOT PRIZE 2,500,000.00

Bank of America   Cashier's Check   No.

JULY 12TH 2010

BANK OF AMERICA LAS VEGAS, NEVADA

Remitter (Purchased By)

Pay *Four hundred and fifty thousand dollars with zero cents $ 450,000.00

To The Order Of   ROBERT ROSS DITTSBURG, PA AN87496

Authorized Signature

Bank of America, N.A.

NOT TRUE CHECKS TO CASH

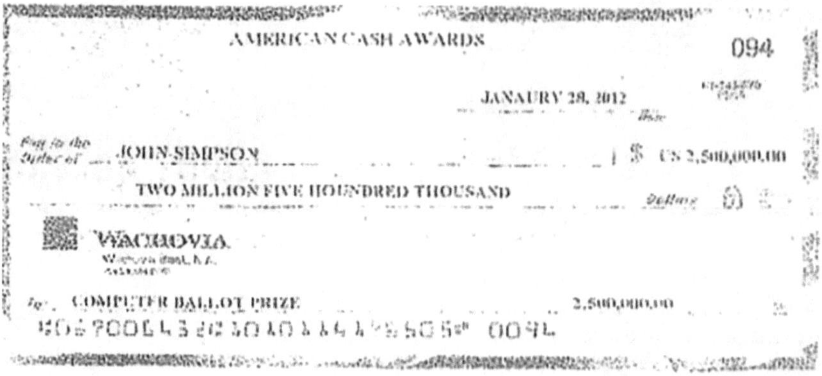

AMERICAN CASH AWARDS

094

JANAURY 28, 2012

Pay to the Order of JOHN SIMPSON $ US 2,500,000.00

TWO MILLION FIVE HOUNDRED THOUSAND   Dollars

WACHOVIA
Wachovia Bank, N.A.

For COMPUTER BALLOT PRIZE   2,500,000.00

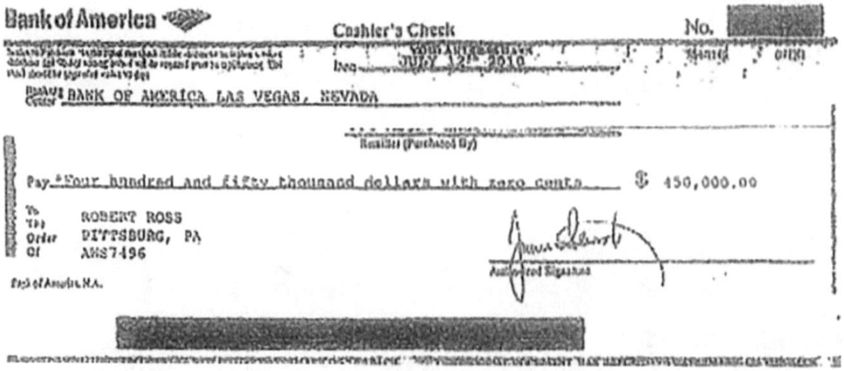

Bank of America   Cashier's Check   No.

JULY 12th 2010

BANK OF AMERICA LAS VEGAS, NEVADA

Remitter (Purchased By)

Pay *Four hundred and fifty thousand dollars with zero cents $ 450,000.00

To The Order Of   ROBERT ROSS
PITTSBURG, PA
AHS7496

Authorized Signature

Bank of America, N.A.

NOT TRUE CHECKS TO CASH

Research about Winning Your Cash Prize

I've done my research on the cash prize that they say you won when they call you. After they call you about your winnings and tell you about it and how to claim it. I've been through this, so I didn't get anything, paid out all the fees they say you won. So I took it deeper. I made a lot of calls to the Trade Commissioner office and told them all about how they use their company name and tell us we won a prize. It's not true about how they can use a company that it's not true. So I made other calls on the big sweepstakes and told them they wanted names and phone numbers, so I gave them all the names and phone numbers to them. They also told me because they are a big sweepstakes company that told me if you won a prize and gifts and any other cash prize they say you won. You shouldn't have to pay out any money out any money out of your pocket and be careful on giving them personal information like SSN, bank account, credit card numbers, e-mail address, license number, or any other information that you have. Once you won a prize, all fees are supposed to be all paid for and stamped of approval, shipping and handling fees, all papers of documents of state to state fees, and any other fees that they ask you to paid for and should be paid for by you. One big part on all the calls that comes in is they all comes from Jamaica and they use a landline phone number that is 1-876-000- 0000. They say things to scam you on getting you to send money to them. I made phone calls to find out how they say things and do all this to the people in USA and use them to get you excited and tell you about your prize with all that doing on my research about your cash prize. Be careful on them calling you because they will keep calling you a lot and ten to twenty times each day and your phone will keep on ringing and ringing until you answer your phone then they will convince you to send even a payment or whatever to get you to send in money to them and lie to you on everything about your prize. Don't believe them at all on doing anything and don't pay out any fees out of your pocket.

Notification of Payment

ACCOUNTS PAYABLE OFFICE
AWARD CONTEST DIVISION

Robert Ross of VA
PO BOX 4894
Virginia Beach, VA 23454-0894

Robert Ross from
Virginia Beach, VA
ID 00051490076

Congratulations successful entrant!

You have been awarded a Check or Cash equivalent in Lieu. We cannot send you your winnings without proper I.D. confirmation.

You must reply to this notice to receive your confirmed funds. Facsimile Check for inspection below. You may be sent actual Check or Cash amount when we receive your request.

Please fill out payment confirmation form on the next page. Again, money has definitely been awarded to you. When we receive s our confirmation, your money will be sent to s our approved address.

Again, congratulations. Please enclose your confirmation fee. payable to N.O.P. and mail it with your confirmation form in the envelope provided within 10 days to secure further entry opportunities in amount of. about or in excess of $2,200,000.00 which have just become known to our legal department for which you are 100% eligible.

Best Wishes and Thank you.
Benjamin James
Accounts Payable Office

March 4, 2014
DATE

PAY TO THE ORDER OF — Robert Ross

$ 15,751.00

SECURITY FEATURES NOT INCLUDED

Fifteen Thousand Seven Hundred and Fifty One Dollars

WARNING

DO NOT ACCEPT THIS CHECK UNLESS YOU SEE A TRUE WATERMARK WHEN HOLDING THE CHECK TO THE LIGHT

MEMO — Congratulations, Robert Ross

Notification of Payment
CASH/PRIZE DOCUMENT   CONSUMER
DATA CONTROL   CONFIRMATION
PROCESSING DEPARTMENT   FORM

CONFIRMATION FORM
NAME: Robert Ross
Address: PO Box 4894
 Virginia Beach, VA 23454-0894

NAME/ADDRESS IS CORRECT   AWARD DOCUMENTATION
CORRECT IF NEEDED   CASH/PRZE INFO
                             REPORTED TO INDIVIDUALS

DELIVERY/RELEASE
AMOUNT IMPRINTD FOR INSPECTION:
* * $ 2,200,000.00 * * *
*** Two Million Two Hundred Thousand Dollars ***

APPROVED PARTICIPANT; I am replying to this notice to confirm my Identity and Delivery Address. The Confirmed data contains the entrant directives and complete entry advisement for the Full Prize on Record. 1 understand winner is required to pay the appropriate taxes on the Awards won. Cash and Prizes are to be paid to the winner by the Individual Sponsor as Reported. I am signing below and am enclosing the requires $20.00 Confirmation data fee as directed. I have inspected the Monies/Prizes Amount as staled here. Delivery to me is direct.

    * * $ 2,200,000.00 * * * Two Million Two Hundred Thousand Dollars
My fee is enclosed as (select) Cash __ Check* __ Money Order__ *made payable to N.O.P. Main Office
THIS DOCUMENT STATES AN ACTUAL CASH/PRIZE RELEASE DATA

RECEIVER: Robert Ross
PO Box 4894
Virginia Beach, VA 23454-0894

X SIGNATURE OF
THE RECEIVER

Signature of Robert Ross

81537

* * * ¢2,200,000.00 00/100 s * * *

NOP Doc 0813-02   Coded and attended by NOP

RESEARCH ABOUT WINNING YOUR CASH PRIZE

That's why it becomes a sweepstakes scam. I'm here to help you out so this won't happen to you and you become broke and your banking account becomes negative in a way that a lot of your bank fees that they cause you to do and they convince you that is already a lie on getting a big prize. (PLEASE DON'T BELIEVE THEM.) Sweepstakes are a prize on a giveaway where the winners are chosen by luck. Prize can range from a small item like cash money, or tickets, to up to house, cars, and enormous prize of a winnings that you don't have to pay out any money or fees.

SAMPLE LETTER ABOUT A CASH PRIZE

ROBERT, You Are A Winner!

NOTIFICATION OF PAYMENT

CONFIRMATION FORM

DELIVERY / RELEASE
AMOUNT SUBMITTED FOR INSPECTION.

*** * * $2,200,000.00 * ***

THIS DOCUMENT STATES AN ACTUAL CASH PRIZE RELEASE DATA

RECEIVER:

X SIGNATURE OF THE RECEIVER _______________
Signature of Robert Ross

PAGE # 24

18

THE DOS AND DON'TS ON WHAT YOU CAN ASK FOR ABOUT YOUR SWEEPSTAKES AND CASH PRIZE

When they call you on your cash prize be very careful. Don't be afraid on what you can ask them everything you want to know about your cash prize. You can ask than to fax you all the information about your cash prize with asking them the Name, Phone Number an other than the 1-876-000-0000 (BE CAREFUL OF THESE NUMBERS.) Try to get a better number and company name, company address. Be careful if the address is out of the USA. (CHECK ALL INFORMATION THAT GETS FAXED TO YOU.) Because 100 percent of it is not true. It could show you a picture on your winning like a new car and show you a picture on your cash money you'll receive (NOT.) Phony checks that has your name on it. It's phony because its scam on their computer that they put your name on it and add up a date. Then their put your phony amount of your millions to it and your check as well. Ask them about how they got your name to their sweepstakes. Remember if you went to a store, mall, or any type of a department store to fill out a sweepstakes entry form or a coupon and put all your personal information on it then you're in the system now. Don't do these anymore because the best way to win is not to enter or play their game of phony sweepstake or paying out a fee for your cash prize that you are not getting anyway. The dos is get all the information that they say on your cash prize. The don'ts is not give diem any information like SSN, license number, bank account, credit card information. Don't let them talk you into anything at all. Do get their name, address, phone number, and keep all this information so keep it for your records. They all work together as a team. Be careful not to play their game. The best way to play is don't play their game; you will lose. I want to put them out of business (IN JAMAICA).

MY EXPERIENCE WITH SWEEPSTAKES AGENT THAT I WENT THROUGH

My Experience with Mr. Phillipe/Mr. Sid Well

I'm writing this letter to you about my prize money that you said I won and let me know I won the prize of $989,000. I did my part on the fee of $2,100 for my prize and to receive it. I've been in some different situation along the way but first I done my research on this and other sweepstakes and lottery winnings look on the Internet and made some important phone calls to people who deals with sweepstakes scams. They're telling me and yes, it's on the Internet and it states once you're a winner on a sweepstakes or lottery, you shouldn't have to pay out of your pocket to receive your prize. Once a sweepstakes try to tell you about a service fee, taxes, etc., then that sweepstakes company is a scam. I've talked with the Federal Trade Commissioner and the Federal Bureau Investigation and a sweepstakes company that deals with people who gets scam on a sweepstakes and they tell me I shouldn't have to pay anything out of my pocket to receive this cash prize that I won. And any company of a sweepstakes out of the USA because like your company you're a scam, and I'm doing research on sweepstakes and put it into a book that I already have about twenty-five to thirty-five sweepstakes company who collect a fee on a person like me to pay out a fee to get a prize I won. Now since you are not letting me have my cash prize of the $989,000 because you want a fee from me so I receive it you are wrong for charging me a fee to get a prize money that I won. (SO I PAY THE FEE TO RECEIVE MY PRIZE AND WAITED AND NOTHING CAME THAT THEY GAVE ME A DATE AND TIME) I also have more than one hundred names since last few years on people who call me and letting me know I won a big cash prize. The prize money should have all fees taken out of it and should not be charge to me to receive my cash prize. I'm writing a book on sweepstakes scam that everyone who has called me and scam me will be in my book that I'm writing out.

I through I was able to receive this cash prize to me and Pm going to add all reason why you have to pay out on a sweepstakes. How to protect yourself on all sweepstakes that charge you a fee and a whole lot more and I guess I will be putting you into my book and all the company and all information. I'm doing more research on my book and hope to have it done real soon and have it out by next year. So if you don't want your name in my book send me my cash prize; if not, then I know this is a scam like all the other company is doing to people. I'm not losing anything either way getting it or not It's all going to be the truth on how sweepstakes works and scams. I'm also trying to go on some talk shows and let the public know not to get into any sweepstakes their all scams. (YES I'VE BEEN SO MAD AT ALL OF THESE SCAMS WHO TAKE MY MONEY AND GET ME NOTHING AS MY PRIZE.) Don't forget my name and I'm going to put all sweepstakes out of business and change everything on sweepstakes out there today. I told them what I was going to do if they didn't pay me my prize money and gave them a chance, but they didn't and time ran out so that's why I'm writing my book. (BE CAREFUL ON SWEEPSTAKES, SCAMS.)

My Experience with Mr. Nathaniel McFarlane / John Mongumery

He called and told me he had a big prize for me and told me how he can help me get it I told him I'd been with a lot of different sweepstakes company and paid out a lot of money, but going nothing in return with my cash prize. He promised me that I didn't have to worry about anything at all, just follow all his direction on how to receive my prize. I told him what was my prize. He told me it was a $2,450,000 check and $50,000 in cash and two new cars, A BIG CREDIT CARD, insurance for the cars that was paid for. It started out with a little amount of my fees that was about $1,500. So I made payments, then after making all the payments, it was my delivery time. Then he told me about making it a rush delivery. I needed to come up with about $400. So I had to make some more payment to get my prize. That was not going to happen on my delivery date. He said, "Don't worry. It will happen." After a few more days, it came back on a small amount of rush delivery amount of $30 to $50 with a total of additional money of $600, and he kept adding more money to it on a grand total of $2,500 and all the additional money I put out on fees from Western Union, international phone cards, and buying Green Dot MoneyPak cards. That was about $200 that I spent to get my prize. So one thing to watch out for when doing a payments through Western Union, all payments goes to Jamaica. Be careful. (THIS ALL COMES DOWN TO A SCAM.) And he changed names and phone numbers. Watch out for the 1-876-number. He makes you think that you'll be dealing with another person that is so phony. He'll tell you all about your winnings, but it adds up to lies. He'll take your money and give back nothing and comes up with excuses on delivery time and date. He also goes to different people that will call you and tell you that everything has been turned over to them. And now it comes to a different money fee that you need to pay and you still get nothing in return.

Don't believe them, and all of them are cowards and con artist that don't show up at your door to give you your prize. At the bottom are names and agents that work with Mr. Mcfarlane that they work or know of sometimes working with him. And the other things to look out for is that they will change their name to throw you off because they want more money from you and they will want you to buy a top-up phone card for them, so you can get your prize sooner. And all it is to put money on their phone to add minutes to their phone so they can scam someone else. They will do anything and say anything to you to con you out of your money.

THESE ARE NAMES THAT HAVE WORKED WITH HIM OR KNOW HIM TOGETHER AS A TEAM

MR. WINTER MR. BROWN MR. WASHINGTON	MR. TAYLOR MR. BELL MR. BEN

My Experience with Mr. Brown

I receive a call telling me I won a big prize. It was $2.5 million and $80,000 in cash. He told me his name was Mr. Brown, he was an agent working on my prize, and what I needed to do to receive it. He told me that there was a percentage that I had to pay to get it. It was about $2,000 and that it was all fees, stamp of approval, and another stamp that goes state to state with storage fees, rush deliver, shipping and handling fee. I told him I didn't have that kind of money for all those fees. He said, "Don't worry we can work out a payment plan each week." Now after making all the payments, he also said, "Make a payment to Western Union," and he'd give me the name to a Merchant Banker that went to their office in Jamaica. I didn't know about all of that at that time. I just wanted to receive my prize. After making all the payments for my cash prize, he told me some additional cost about running all paperwork and documents. So I paid from $200 to $300 to take care of more final paperwork and to have the delivery to my house, and he had to call the delivery guys to make arrangements. This took a few days. After waiting a few days, he called me back. There were a little more fees for shipping and handling. He told me it was about $200. Then as soon as I took care of the fee, it would take two days to come to my house for my prize. I told him I didn't have enough money at that time. I didn't have any more fees. He told me, "Don't worry about the fees this time." He told me to go out and get a Green Dot MoneyPak card. "You can go to Walmart, Kmart, or any other drug store to get this card." So I paid all the money ($3,500 total) out of my pocket. Then he told me to get ready for my delivery date and time in two to three days. He told me that they would call for an address and the time to make sure I was home. After about two days, I heard nothing and tried calling him and got no answer. (BE CAREFUL OF THE NUMBERS OF 1-876-000-000.) So I went out and got an international phone card and called him. I got no answer from him. He finally answered and told me he was coming, but he gave me some excuse like the car broke down, got into an accident, or a lot of different stories and excuses.s I heard them all.

My Experience with Mr. Omar

This guy said he can help me out to get my cash prize if I can do some work for him and he'll make sure I will get my prize. He asks me if I can pick up a package in California from this lady so she can get her prize. He told me I didn't have to pay out anything out of my pocket to work with him and take a trip to California to pick up the package and send it back to him. He said that he will pay for the trip to California and put me on a private plane and meet the lady at the airport; she is to meet me at there and put me on the plane to California. The lady's name is Nancy and part of the money that I'm picking up from California was to pay the pilot part of the money. So I went to the airport to meet Nancy where I was supposed to meet her at a location like Omar said, and I waited, no Nancy—not even a phone call that Omar said she was going to call me. Once I got to the airport, he called me and he asked me that I was supposed to pay into the trip. I said, "I thought you were going to pay for the trip for me to go to California and pick up the money." (I FOUND OUT A LOT OF REASON WHY HE WANTED ME TO DO THAT FOR HIM AND HOW HE WAS SCAMMING THE LADY IN CALIFORNIA AND STARTED TO SCAM ME ALSO.) He told me how Nancy needed $390 for part of the plane ticket, and Omar told me he paid over $1,100 for plane ticket. And I told him I didn't have the money to pay for the trip. I asked him, "You said it wasn't going to cost me any money for the trip." He told me, "I can make a commission on it and if I pay into it for the trip and pay part of the cost of the plane ticket, I could get paid on the commission for doing that for him. (I THINK HE WAS TRYING, AND HE DIDN'T.) He kept telling me no games are being played. I'd been going to the airport about three to five times in about a few weeks at that time, and I hadn't seen Nancy, not once since I'd been going to the airport and was supposed to meet her at the main gate to put me on the plane. I told him if the trip was true, I'd like to have the lady from California's number so I could talk to her and pick up the package.

Now Omar keeps asking me to pay out more money on this trip and after I paid my money to him, he already payed the ticket, and I thought he was scamming me for money. I talked with the lady in California, her name is Dorothy she said she has $100,000 cash for me to be picked up and by that time, I left for the airport (AT THIS POINT I HAD TALKED WITH DOROTHY TO FIND OUT IF IT WAS TRUE ABOUT PICKING UP THE CASH MONEY IN CALIFORNIA) The next time he called me and told me, "Did you talk with the lady (DOROTHY)?" and I said she has the money. He called me when I got to the airport and asked me, "Can you get up additional money for additional purchase of the cost for the ticket?" (I THINK THERE IS STILL SOMETHING GOING ON) I told him I paid the money for the ticket. I don't have any more money on me. He said, "Don't worry. You'll get your commission out of the money. (NORDIA REID) After I do this, you can go back to the airport" (THIS WAS ABOUT THE FOURTH TIME TO GO TO THE AIRPORT AND NOT EVEN GET TO THE PLANE) "and wait for Nancy to get me on the plane." I asked him, "Are you sure this time you will make it to the plane and make the trip to California?" So I went back to the airport, and I waited for about an hour, then I got a call, telling me the name changed because the person was not able to pick up the money.

BAD PEOPLE TO DEAL WITH
MR. OMAR = NORDIA REID = MR. BLACK

Be very careful who you talk to because these guys will scam you in a lot of different ways to get your money out of your bank account and your credit cards. But remember you will pay and pay all your money to them until you are broke and you think you're getting a prize you're not. I'm here to let you know on my experience that Omar and all the other guys working with him will scam you and even if you do a Western Union and Money Gram. They will tell you they have offices here in the USA but there is not one office here. It all goes to Jamaica. Nancy hasn't called me, and I haven't seen her. Omar said she was busy and just wait a little more time she well be there to meet me. I took it on my own and called Dorothy back and asked her if she has the cash and she said yes it was $100,000, and I asked who was picking it up. I told her that Omar still wanted me to pick it up. Omar was making arrangements to get me on the plane, but it was not working out so I told him I'll drive there to pick it up. I waited two days and called her back; she then told me the truth about everything and how she paid out $200 a few months ago and it drained her banking account negative with no money in it. He and Mr. Black conned you out on different things like sending out money to Western Union. They tell you to go out and buy a Green Dot MoneyPak card, he even said, "It's about your prize, but after you pay all the fees, another guy will call, and he'll tell you about a delivery fee, state sticker fee, and they will add more that you have to pay out." Don't believe them at all.

My Experience with James Taylor

He called me and said he and a few guys would do the delivery of my prize of $18.5 million and a new 2011 BMW that they say I won. I told him to meet me at the address I gave him. We set up a time to meet. The time was 1:00 p.m. I got there, waited for about an hour—no show. I gave him a call, no answer. So I was mad and I went home because no one showed up. (I HAD TO GO OUT AND BUY AN INTERNATIONAL PHONE CARD TO CALL THE 1-876-000-0000). Then a couple of days went by, he called me. "Got another phone call now," he said, "another thing came up." I asked him, "What now?" He was trying to come and deliver my prize, but another thing came up, and it was another additional fee, and he will call me back and give me the information on it. (I FEEL THAT THEY KEPT GIVING ME EXCUSES LIKE THE CAR BROKE DOWN AND A FLAT TIRE DURING THE TRIP TO MY HOUSE.) So the call came in, now he told me to put $325 on a Green Dot MoneyPak card. I told him, "I don't do it that way. I put it on my debit card and told him to be there the next day and meet between 1:30 p.m. and 2:00 p.m. and "I'm not going to put out any more money and any information to you over the phone like my additional card until I see you in person." He could see that I give him the number of my debit card already for payment. I felt that he wasn't far from the location to meet, and he called me on a 1-876-000-0000 number that comes from Jamaica. (I DID MY RESEARCH ON THE 1-876 AND IT COMES FROM JAMAICA). So after all this planning and giving him money to receive my prize, I know he wasn't coming to deliver my prize because he was still in Jamaica. So this made me mad so it's time to put all the information that I had from him and everyone else to do the research on this sweepstakes from other companies and collect phone numbers and put it in a book one day. After a few days and putting this together, I went out and got an international phone card and called him back. It took me a few times to reach him, and I told him, "Mr. Taylor, what I'm going to do and what I found out through my research on this sweepstakes that if I didn't get my prize that you have for me, I'll put a stop to it and put your name on my bad list of scammers and put it in a book."

He has different guys working with him and play different parts of your prize. Don't believe them they all work together. They will also ask you to put money on their phone bill (IT'S A TOP-UP CARD THAT ADDS MINUTES TO THEIR PHONE) to add minutes to their phone so you can get your prize (DON'T DO THIS, YOU WON'T GET NOTHING IN RETURN AND YOU WON'T GET YOUR PRIZE ALL LIES.)
THESE ARE THE GUYS WHO WORK TOGETHER TO SAY

YOU'RE GETTING A PRIZE

TAYLOR/PETERSON = THEY ARE BROTHERS
JOHN BEN = HE'S THEIR COUSIN
DAVE WASHINGTON = HE'S THEIR FRIEND

MY EXPERIENCE WITH JAMES TAYLOR / JOHN BEN

These two guys are cousins that work together as a team. They get you to believe if you work for them, you can make extra money or get your prize faster, but it all goes back to them. They will tell you if you put money on their phone and buy one of the top- up card to add minutes they will make sure you can reduce your fee for your prize, but not true. They are just like con artist and all want your money and make you broke in your bank account and credit cards.

20

START DOING A TELEMARKETING AND CALLING USING CELL PHONE NUMBERS ON YOUR CASH PRIZE

These sweepstakes company, as they say that there are not any good company but, they are not any good sweepstakes out there. They are using different companies and names, calling you like a telemarketing companies do. They use a calling systems to get phone numbers and even cell phone. They will call you and tell you that you won a big cash prize. Don't believe it, but go with what I'm saying in my book from other chapters and use it as a guidebook. These calls all comes from Jamaica and use a 1-876-000-0000 be careful on these numbers and any other calls that comes in on a sweepstakes. Be careful as the telemarketing systems that are out there today and how they use you when they call you and get you excited on your prize. The telemarketing and sweepstakes that they use the same concept and try to get you to send money in another country like Jamaica that they are in an office building with other and use each other for you to send money to Western Union or the Money Gram. Like the telemarketing do in a big room and they use a phone system and a computer system as well. Be careful not to give them information about you. And when you quit answer the phone they will even call you twenty to thirty times again and again they will call a call you just to scam you on your cash prize. And they will try to get you to sign up with an international phone system and you pay a fee to get started with a little fee every minute. This is a phone service from Jamaica be careful on this service. If you have caller ID on your phone service and these numbers comes up as a 1-876-000-0000 than don't answer these calls because once you do this they won't leave you alone and they will trick you to pay out a fee and send it to Jamaica on your cash prize. I'm here to protect you so you won't make the mistake like I did and lost a lot of money to get my cash prize, but that's why I'm writing this book to help you out so you won't lose your money over them about a Sweepstakes. I'm here to let you know I started to believe them at first and got con in their game. Don't do this; the only way to win a sweepstakes is not to play. You'll be a big winner once you don't play their scam game and the other best way to win is to play die lottery.

21

ALL ABOUT JAMAICA, 1-876, INTERNATIONAL PHONE CARD, AND TOP-UP CARD

Jamaica is a small country down south. They use a system to call you on your prize and all calls comes from Jamaica. Don't believe them. They tell all lies to you, and we'll learn about it in my book They know that the only way to get money and to make a living in their country is to scam us out of our hard-earned money and use a system like the sweepstakes that you're not going to get anyway. The only way they can make a living is by taking people's money. Learn not to give your money out to them and don't let them think that the American people is smarter than giving away your money that they're not getting a prize back. (DON'T DO THIS ANYMORE. I'M HERE TO SAVE YOU THOUSANDS AND THOUSANDS OF DOLLARS THAT YOU CAN SAVE IN YOUR POCKET.) And watch out for the 1-876-000-0000 number; they use this to call you a lot. It's the number that comes from Jamaica and it's a landline number, and this number, 1-876, is how they call you from another country. And if you need to call them back, you can go out and buy an international phone card. It's a 1-877 or a 1-866 number and call this put in the pin number and then call the 1-876 number to call back then, scammers be very careful. And they will talk you into putting minutes on their phone and tell you to go to the drug store buy the (TOP-UP PHONE CARD.) You can call the number on the card put in the pin and do what the top up card tells you to do and add the phone number they give you to add minutes. (BUT ALL THIS IS TO HELP PAY FOR THEIR PHONE AND TO SCAM SOMEONE ELSE AND TO TELL YOU THIS IS FOR YOUR PRIZE THAT THEY HAVE TO MAKE CALLS ON ITS ALL LIES DON'T BELIEVE THEM ON THIS.) If you do this for them, they will tell you it will help you out to receive all your prize money faster, but it won't they just want to get more money out of your pocket to take more of your time. But, with all that I said you spend all your money and time to receive your prize. But in all the world today there is not one sweepstakes company that is not going to give you a prize.

22

SWEEPSTAKES AND TELEMARKETERS

To my friends, I'm here to help you out and you don't get scammed anymore and what I've been doing on my research and letting you know about my research on telemarketers calling you and trying to say you're a winner of a prize and get you an offer of a special price on magazines that you're not going to read at all, and you pay out money each month for the payment of the magazines. And you will get wrong ones that you didn't ask for from the beginning when you ordered them. (LOOK OUT FOR THIS BECAUSE I DIDN'T GET ANY OF THE MAGAZINE THAT I ASKED FOR. TRY TO CALL IT IN AND TELL THEM ABOUT THE MISTAKE. IT TOOK ME A FEW TIMES ON THE PHONE AND IT NEVER GOT THE RIGHT ANSWER. WHEN I TALK TO THE MAIN PERSON, THEY TRY TO GET THE RIGHT MAGAZINE ORDER. THEY SAID IT WILL BE CORRECTED, BUT AFTER A FEW WEEKS, THEY STILL COME IN THE MAIL, ALL WRONG AGAIN SO I STILL DIDN'T GET THE RIGHT MAGAZINE. BUT I GOT TO CANCEL MY CREDIT CARD.) And you're going to be in a drawing for the sweepstakes that they say you're going to win. All they want is your money to buy magazines that you're not going to read; it's all a waste of time and money. Save your money and go to the store to buy your favor magazines. It's cheaper in the long run. And sometimes you'll receive a post card in the mail saying you won a different prize for free, but you have ten days to call it in and then they get you on the shipping and handling fee so you can receive your prize. Once they get you on the phone, they tell you it will only take a minute to get all your information and address so you can get your prize. They will want a credit card so you can pay for the shipping and handling fee. And then they will give you and extra free gift like a dinner card to your favorite restaurant that they will add it to your order, and it's only a few more dollars to receive your $25 dinner card.

Once you approve of all this, they will tell you that you get another gift item such as free gas card for a year just to get your approval on it, but it's going to cost you more on your credit card (YOU CAN FIGURE IT OUT) in the long run, and you can add it up. It's going to cost you more money for all your free gifts. So where is this all free? It will cost you.

TELEMARKETERS # WHY THEY CALL YOU
    (1)   They get you to join for a cash prize of about $10,000 to $15,000.

        And once they get you into a sweepstakes of their own, they get you to order magazines that you don't need.
    (2)   They charge you more than what you can get from them at the store.
    (3)   They charge your credit card on a monthly fee that after a few months it adds up to around $69.00 to $83.00 or more, and you're paying 4 to 5 times the above or the price in the store.
    (4)   They say this is a prize, but it's all a big cost to you.

ALL ABOUT PHONY AND PAYDAY LOANS

These guys call me up and said, "You got approved on a loan," and I said, "What kind of a loan?" He said, "It's a payday loan to help you out." I told him I wasn't in or looking into getting a payday loan. He said, "We have a good rate." So they are just like a scam or like any other sweepstakes that they want you to get. I went ahead on talking with him more on this payday loan. He said if I get a loan from $2,500 to $5,000 loan that day, the rate will be low.

I try to get him on the rate of the loan, but he went on and tell me about the payment on each month would be on the loan. I ask him on what monthly payment will it be and he said, "What amount on the loan are you looking to have?" I told him, "How about the $2,500 loan amount?" He said, "Why don't you go for the $5,000 loan. I told him I only have a little amount each month to do a loan. And after we do the paperwork, how long would it take to receive the loan in my account? He said we do it and a payout would be through Western Union. I ask him why do I have to pay out the loan thru Western Union, he said its faster that why. "How much information do you need from me?" He said, "Not much." He said, "In order for you to receive this loan amount, you have to pay your monthly service amount and your monthly payment up front."

"How much do you need for the service fee and monthly payment?"

"He said in between $350 to $400." I said, "Why would I have to pay up front money first on a payday loan?" He said, "To cover the service fee and application fee and monthly fee." If I had that money right now, I wouldn't have to do a payday loan, and how many payment would it take to pay it off. He said, "Start out with the first payment of $400 for the first twelve months, then do a payment of $350 for the rest of the months until it's paid off. And if you do the higher amount of a loan, it's going to be about a payment of $500 to $600 and about eighteen months to twenty-four months to pay it off on the loan." I told him this does not sound good to do monthly payment to get a loan. I told him, "I don't know where you have the right to charge people an upfront payment and service fee to get a loan." So after I got off the phone, I did a test each on a real payday loan place. She told me, "It's after you do the loan your payment would start thirty days, and we accept your application to do the loan first." (SO WATCH THESE, GUYS, CALLING YOU ON A LOAN, AND THEY ARE SCAMMERS ABOUT THIS.)

PHONY COMPANIES THAT SENDS YOU LETTERS COMPANY NAMES AND ADDRESSES

This company sends you out a letter and tell you, you are a winner of a sweepstakes that you entered. Once you read the letter and the amount that is on die letter saying you'll be a winner of $2.5 million to $10.5 million and all you have to do is send the amount that could be from $9.95 to $39.95 and send this in with your entry form so you can be a winner of the prize that is going to be awarded to you. Once you send it in with die small amount and your entry form, you'll a winner. Someone will call you and tell you how to claim it and what to do next to receive it (I DID THIS AND SENT IN THE AMOUNT AND ENTRY FORM TO RECEIVE MY CASH AMOUNT THAT I WON AND I WAITED FOR IT TO COME AND THE PERSON DIDN'T CALL ME BACK. ALL THEY WANTED IS MY MONEY AND NO PRIZE ANYWAY. PLEASE REMEMBER IF IT SOUNDS GOOD TO BE TRUE AND EASY TO GET IT AND YOU PAY OUT MONEY TO RECEIVE A CASH PRIZE—IT'S NOT TRUE. SO BE CAREFUL AND DON'T PLAY THEIR GAME. IT'S CHEAPER NOT TO ENTER AND PAY OUT ANYTHING AT ALL. SAVE YOUR

MONEY AND BE BETTER OFF ON PLAYING THE LOTTERY DO NOT ENTER IN A SWEEPSTAKES AND LOSE YOUR MONEY WHEN YOU SEND IT TO THEM WITH ALL THESE COMPANIES. YOU'RE NOT A WINNER ANYWAY AND I AM HERE TO SAVE YOU THOUSANDS AND THOUSANDS OF DOLLARS NOT TO ENTER IN ANY SWEEPSTAKES THAT THEY WANT YOU TO PAY INTO—A CASH PRIZE AND DIFFERENT ITEMS. THAT'S WHY I DID THIS GUIDE BOOK TO SAVE YOU. I'M TIRED OF DOING THIS AND PAYING OUT THE FEES AND SENDING IT IN AND THEY WILL TELL YOU YOU'RE A WINNER. I DID THIS AND ONE TIME. AND ONCE I GOT IN THE MAIL I SENT IT OUT THAT DAY. BUT GOT NOTHING. IT'S JUST A WASTE OF MONEY AND TIME. (PLEASE DON'T FALL FOR ANY SWEEPSTAKES. YOU'RE GOING TO LOSE ANYWAY.)

COMPANY NAMES AND ADDRESSES

PROCESSING DEPT
GLOBAL REPORTING
NETWORK
P.O.BOX 4500
CORONA, CA 92878 - 4500

PROCESSING CENTER
P. O. BOX 3905

LAS VEGAS, NV
89127 – 3905

THE SWEEPSTAKES NOTIFICATION CENTER
PRIZE ELIGIBILITY PROCESSING P.O.BOX 549012
DALLAS, TX 75354 - 9012

NUMEROLOGICAL
RESOURCE CENTER
ANALYSIS DIVISION
P.O.BOX 868
LYNBROOK, NY 11563 - 0868

M P N S

P.O. BOX 9005
BALDWIN, NY
11510 - 9005

PRIZE REGISTRY BUREAU
P.O.BOX 98989
LAS VEGAS, NV 89193- 8989

DMI PRIZE
1525 CAPITAL DR # 109
CARROLLTON, TX
75008 - 3667

VANGUARD DOCUMENTING AGENCY   S.R.C.
P. O. BOX 4500   P. O. BOX 29170
CORONA, CA 92878 - 4500   SHAWNEE MISSION, KS
                                66201

NATIONAL BUREAU DATA DOCUMENTATION
P.O.BOX 29171
SHAWNEE MISSION. KS 66201

Company Names and Addresses

SWEEPSTAKES CLEARING HOUSE
1555 REGAL ROW DALLAS, TX 75247 - 3662

LAS VEGAS ENTERTAINMENT INC
PO BOX 570685
LAS VEGAS, NV 89157

AWARD PROCESSING CENTER
1401 ARMOUR ROAD
PO BOX 219620
KANSAS CITY, MO 64121 - 9620

SWEEPSTAKES PRIZE ENTRY CENTER
PO BOX 549012
DALLAS, TX 75354 - 9012

AMERICAN SWEEPSTAKES PUBLISHER
DEPARTMENT OF PRIZE DATA INFORMATION
PO BOX 29171
SHAWNEE MISSION, KS 66201 - 9171

NATIONAL FINANCIAL GROUP
PO BOX 10150
WILMINGTON, DE 19850-0150

WORLD WIDE AWARD GROUP
PO BOX 9503
MASSAPEQUA, NY 11758-9503

Company Names and Addresses

DOCUMENTATION DELIVERY DIVISION
AMERICAN SWEEPSTAKES PUBLISHER
PO BOX 29171
SHAWNEE MISSION, KS 66201

INT BUSINESS REPLY SERVICE
I.B.R.S./ C.C.R. LNUMERO 10650
1000 RA AMSTERDAM PAYS - BAS

COLUMBIA CLEARING HOUSE
382 CHANNEL DRIVE
PORT WASHINGTON, NY 11050

PRIZE SEARCH NETWORK
PROCESSING CENTER
PO BOX 3905
LAS VEGAS, NV 89127 – 3905

MERRICK PRIZE NOTIFICATION SERVICE
PO BOX 9005
BALDWIN, NY 11510 - 9005

CUSTOMER SERVICE
6170 WESTLAKE MEAD #045
LAS VEGAS. NV 89108 - 2661

PROCESSING DEPT
GLOBAL REPORTING NETWORK
PO BOX 4500
CORONA, CA 92878 - 4500

Company Names and Addresses

CONTEST AMERICAN PUBLISHERS, INC
1401 ARMOUR RD
NORTH KANSAS CITY, MO 64116

PLATINUM PRIZE GROUP
PO BOX 9503
MASSAPEQUA, NY 11758

CERTIFIED PRIZE SLIP REMITTANCE
PO BOX 6119
ST LOUIS, MO 63139 - 0119

NSN PRODUCTS, LLC
3675S RAINBOW BLVD. #107-177
LAS VEGAS, NV 89103

AWARD NOTIFICATION COMMISSION
PO BOX 2902
KANSAS CITY, KS 66110-2902

C.P.R.D.
28 EAST JACKSON BLDG SUITE #1020
CHICAGO, IL 60604 - 2263

CONFIRMED DECLARATION
9101W. SAHARA AYE SUITE # 105 - D27
LAS VEGAS, NV 89117

CHAPTER COMPANYS THAT SEND YOU LETTERS
COMPANYS NAMES & ADDRESS

CHAPTER # 23

RESEARCH DEPARTMENT
GOLD COAST MC QLD 9726
AUSTRALIA

MERCHANDISE DISCOUNT FACILITY
10330 CENTRAL AVE SUITE #327
MONTCLAIR, CA 91783 - 4401

$10,000.00 PRIZE INSURANCE
DPOA
PO BOX 21817
ST LOUIS, MO 63109 - 0817

PRIZE AMERICA
CASH PRIZE PAYMENT OFFICE
P O BOX 9020
AMITYVILLE, NY 11701-9020

PMA GLOBAL INC PMB145
565 PLAN DOME RD
MANHASSET, NY 11030

D.O.C.D.
PO BOX 9005
BALDWIN, NY 11510 - 9005

Company Names and Addresses

CEC
CASH AWARDS DIVISION
PO BOX 5503
MASSAPEQUA, NY 11758-9503

NATIONAL SELECTION SERVICE
PO BOX 9005
BALDWIN, NY 11510-9005

ENTITLEMENT ADVISORY
PO BOX 3905
LAS VEGAS, NV 89127 - 3905

INTERNATIONAL PAYMENT CENTRE
PO BOX 294
LAKE GROVE, NY 11755 - 0294

INTERNATIONAL PAYMENT CENTRE
PO BOX 875.
GIBRALTAR, NY 11755 - 0875

R.O.M.
1383 6TH AVE SUITE #377
NEW YORK, NY 10019 - 3910

ABOUT THE AUTHOR

Hi, friends. Robert Ross has dealt with this for about seven years and he has been getting calls and letters on a lot of different guys on a lot of different scams, and so he did his research on all that he finds out and he did work with them and his experience on all these sweepstakes scams. He got calls from 1-876 number and letters that he played out to receive a prize, but all it did was make him broke with his bank account and credit card going into the negative so that's why he did this guide book on sweepstakes scams so people can learn not to do and save their money. He put everything together so everyone who reads his book can protect themselves on all those scammers that ate out their today so they won't get scammed and lose all their money, and he will save people thousands and thousands of dollars. He knows what he learned that there is no sweepstakes out there because if there was, he would have been in between a millionaire or billionaire. But it never happens that's why all the letters and all the calls and he got were dead information that he collected and he puts it together and put it in this book so people can learn what he has been through dealing with all the lies that they tell you that you're a winner on a cash prize. And yes, he experienced all of those and it's true. This book well help people out a lot for all the dos and don'ts and what to do when they call and explain to how to claim it and all the not-true fees. So please don't give them out any personal information like bank account, credit cards, SSN, license number, or e-mail address. Watch out for these guys from Jamaica, they will scam you on anything that they call you on. Remember that once one fills out an entry form at the mall or a department store, restaurant, and fill out all the information on it and then it goes out to a mailing list, that gets sold to different places and one would think he/she is getting a prize soon, and all the prize that they say one is going to receive would be a new car, new home, cash money, vacation, big money on a credit card, new computer, etc.

Robert Ross